essential careers™

Careers in Glasswork

Tamra B. Orr

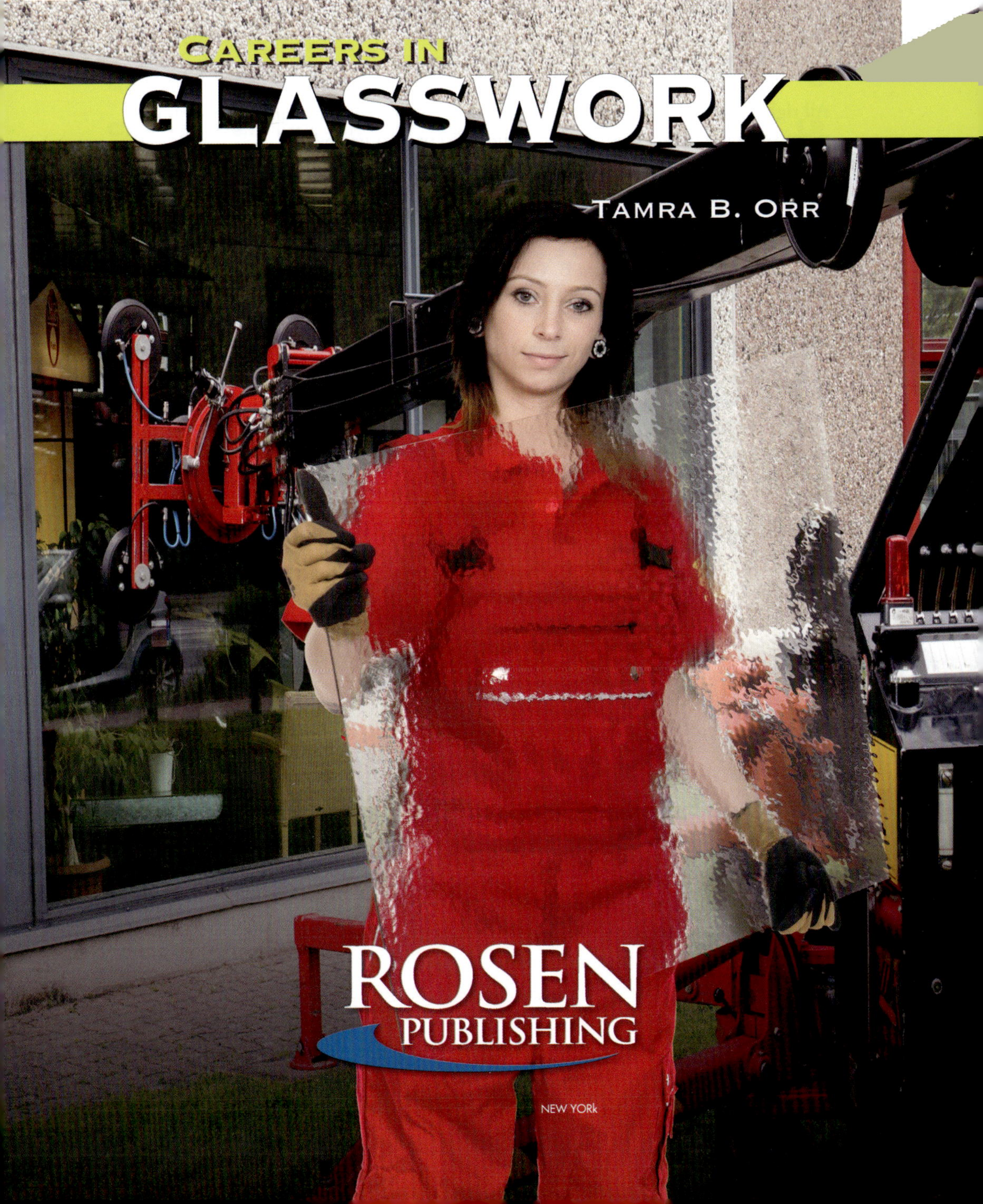

Rosen Publishing
New York

INTRO

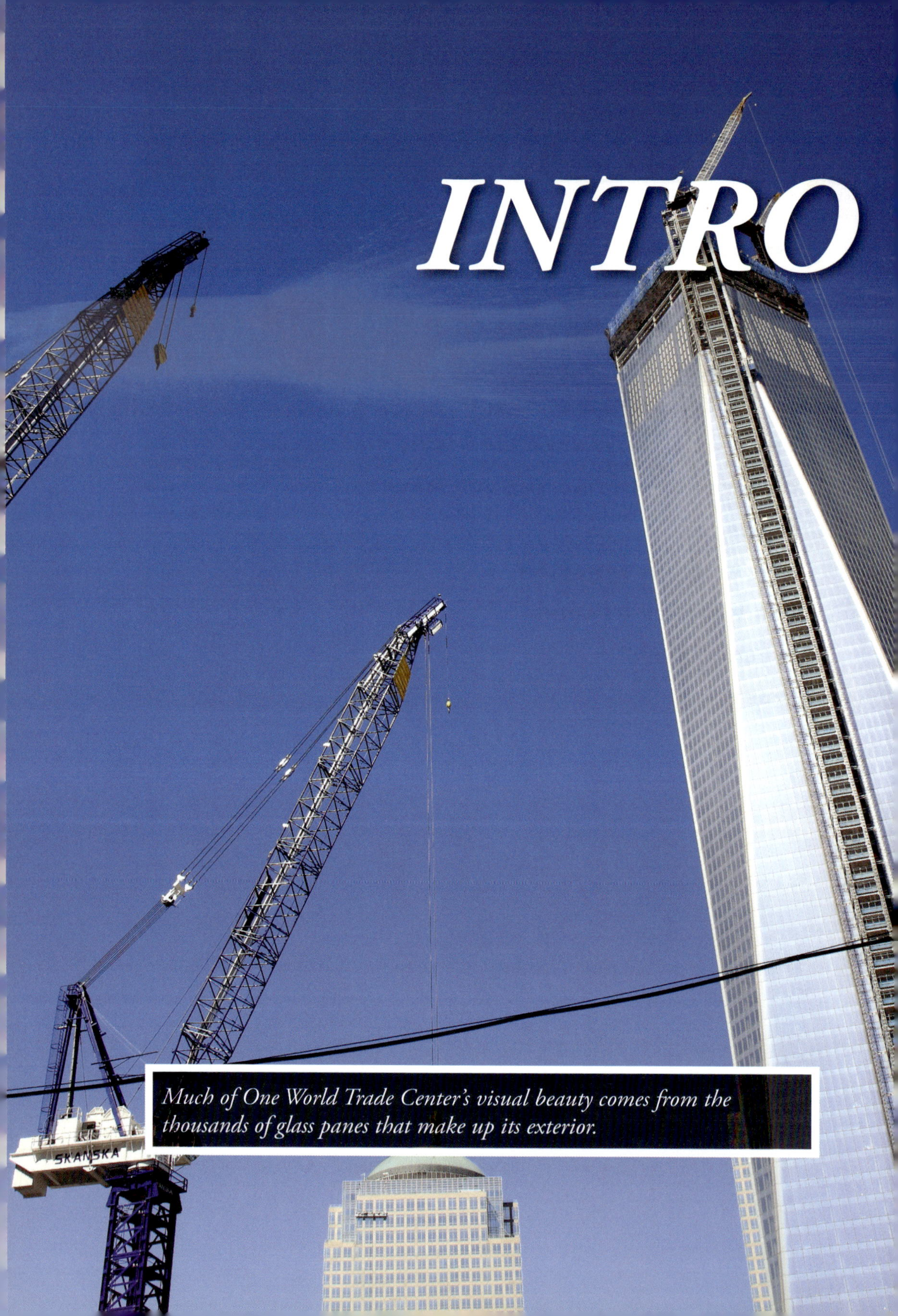

Much of One World Trade Center's visual beauty comes from the thousands of glass panes that make up its exterior.

essential careers™

CAREERS IN GLASSWORK

TAMRA B. ORR

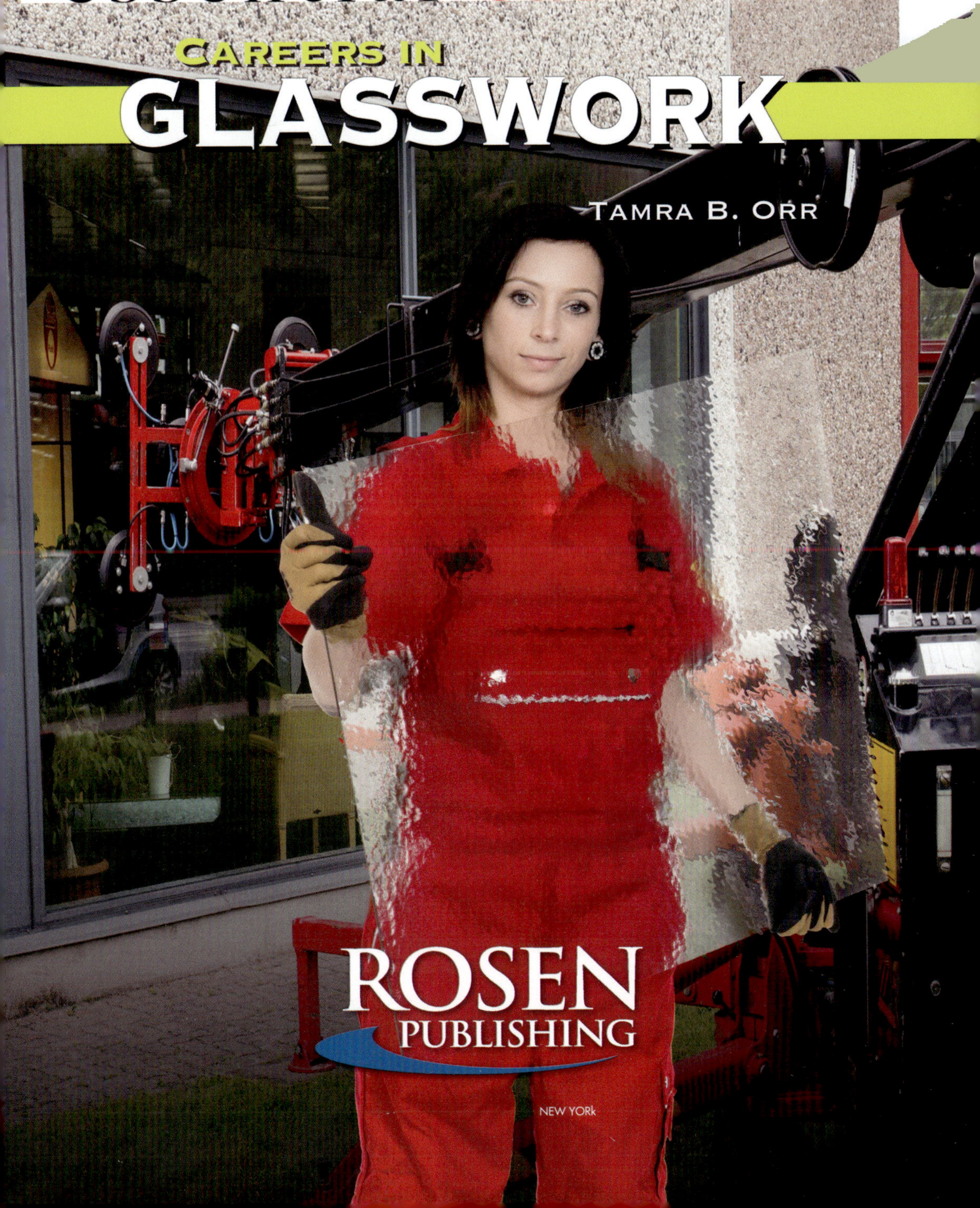

ROSEN PUBLISHING

NEW YORK

Published in 2016 by The Rosen Publishing Group, Inc.
29 East 21st Street, New York, NY 10010

First Edition

Library of Congress Cataloging-in-Publication Data

Orr, Tamra.
Careers in glasswork / Tamra B. Orr. — First edition.
pages cm. — (Essential careers)
Audience: Grades 7–12.
Includes bibliographical references and index.
ISBN 978-1-4994-6211-1 (library bound)
1. Glass manufacture—Vocational guidance—Juvenile literature. I. Title.
TP857.3.O67 2016
666›.1—dc23

2015025838

Manufactured in the United States of America

contents

INTRO

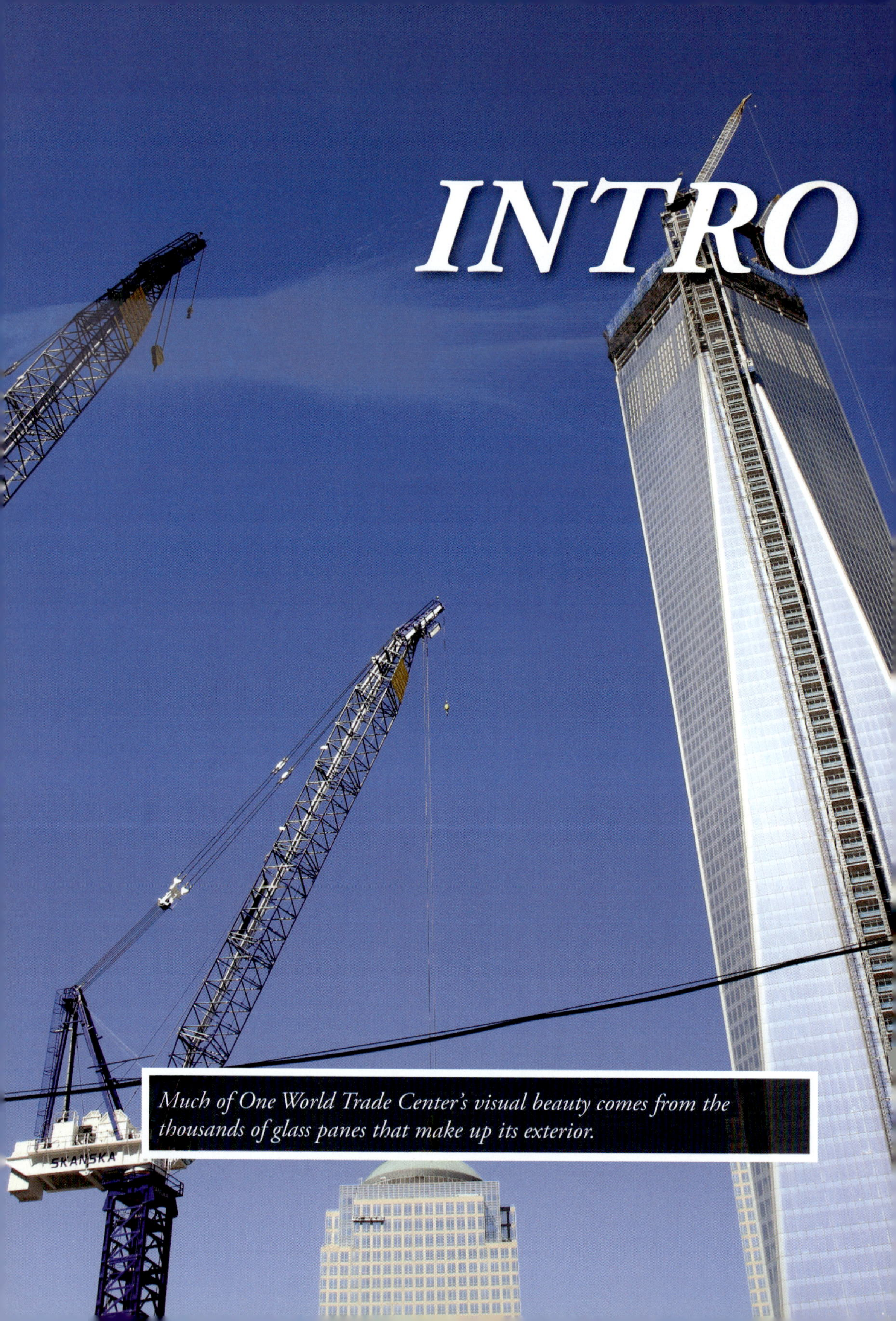

Much of One World Trade Center's visual beauty comes from the thousands of glass panes that make up its exterior.

DUCTION

Colloquially known as the Freedom Tower, One World Trade Center is an incredible structure. It stands at 1,776 feet (541 meters)—a reference to the year the Declaration of Independence was signed. The skyscraper is made of enough concrete to pave more than four thousand city blocks. That concrete is specially designed to withstand seven times more pressure than standard concrete and meets all building safety code standards. The tower also includes two tridents from the original World Trade Center towers, which were lost in the terrorist attacks of September 11, 2001. One World Trade Center also has just shy of 1,000,000 square feet (93,000 square meters) of glass that shines over downtown New York City. That means glaziers—artisans who cut and install glass—were an essential part of constructing this historic building and its seemingly endless walls of windows.

When John Shipman, the director of quality control and project superintendent for Benson Industries, was asked to work on the glass that would be installed on One World Trade Center, it was a wonderful moment. Shipman knows glass. He has worked for Benson Industries for more than thirty-eight years. He has worked on a fifty-five-story hospital in Chicago, Illinois, the Chrysler headquarters in Detroit, Michigan, and two city towers in Seattle, Washington. In 2007, Shipman's company was asked to assemble the huge glass panels for One World Trade Center. "We did the main flat walls at our Gresham, Oregon, location," Shipman said during a phone interview in June 2015. The manufactured glass was then sent to New York to be placed on the building. Shipman spent three years working on the project. "All our work is finish work, out where the public will see it."

More than three thousand large glass panels were used on One World Trade Center. Glaziers worked closely with ironworkers to hoist the heavy panels of glass into place hundreds of feet above the ground. They used state-of-the-art technology, such as a remote control to help control the panels and align them into place. "The workers would bring the panel up, trolley the hoist over," said Ken Barnett, head of national sales at Beta Max Hoist, Inc. (the company that provided the material hoist lifts for One World Trade Center's construction), in an August 2013 article in *Glass Magazine*. "The workers handling the panel had control right there and could carefully put the panel into place. Once in place, they repeated the process, starting again at the staging area."

One World Trade Center is an incredible structure, but the curtain wall of glass on it is just one example of what glassworkers do. Look around you. Try and count all the examples of glass that you see. Chances are that most of it was installed by a glazier. Some glaziers do residential work, completing projects inside homes such as installing windows, tabletops, glass doors, and mirrors. Others work on commercial projects, installing security and display windows, storefronts, room dividers, or the windshields on vehicles, trains, and planes. They also install the glass windows on office buildings, hotels, and towers. Glass is pretty much everywhere!

Glaziers make homes and buildings warmer in the winter and cooler in the summer by providing insulation from weather. They install glass to provide security, sound control, and beauty. “Becoming a glazier gives young people a tremendous opportunity to learn a truly diverse trade,” stated Shipman. “They can do everything from replacing storefront windows to working on skyscrapers—or World Trade Centers. Truly, the sky is the limit!”

chapter 1

A World of Glass

Take a moment to walk around your house and count how many examples of glass you see. First, there are the easy ones to spot—windows, sliding glass doors, shower doors, and mirrors. Don't stop there, though. How about tabletops, cabinetry, front doors, skylights, or display cases? But wait. Don't forget about your electronics. Your cell phone, laptop, tablet, e-reader, television, and computer monitors are all covered in glass, too. All of these are examples of residential glass.

Now imagine taking a walk into your town or city. Are there large storefront windows on department stores, auto dealerships, public libraries, and other businesses? Are there any huge office buildings covered in hundreds of windows? These are examples of commercial glass.

Hold on! Look around again. How many windows and windshields pass by you on cars, trucks, and buses? These are examples of automotive glass.

Glass has many purposes, of course. It can keep the heat of the summer and the chill of the winter outside by providing insulation. It can protect people from wind, rain, or snow. (Think what it would be like to live in a house or ride in a car

Glass workers install the large window frames on houses and other new buildings during the construction process.

without windows!) It can block noise but let in the sunshine. It can reflect images, making driving much safer and getting ready in the morning much easier. Glass provides security and, at the same time, offers great beauty.

Glass also makes up a significant part of any vehicle. Clear glass windows and windshields protect passengers from the weather. Reflective glass in the side and rearview mirrors helps drivers keep track of what is behind and beside them.

THE WORK OF A GLAZIER

There's no question about it. Glass is everywhere—and that means that the people who know how to carry, cut, shape, and install glass are in demand. A glazier (pronounced "glay-zher" where the "-zher" sounds like the "-sure" in "measure") is an expert in how to handle glass, from small, fragile pieces being placed in a fancy door to a huge, thick pane of glass taller than a person and weighing hundreds of pounds. If you have ever dropped a drinking glass or broken a window, you know how easily glass can shatter. Learning how to work with glass without cracking or breaking it is a real skill—and one that takes a lot of practice.

Glaziers work in small home remodeling businesses as well as in huge construction companies. Sometimes they work alone, but more often, they work as part of a team. While some work indoors, most glaziers end up working outdoors in all kinds of weather. Materials and equipment are heavy, and it takes a great deal of strength in order to do some projects. In an online profile of the best jobs in construction, Greg Renne, former glazier and administrator of a

INSIDE A GLASS FACTORY A CENTURY AGO

Glasswork has made major progress with technology in the past hundred years. To get an idea of how far glasswork has come, one only needs to look back at a typical glass factory just a century ago. According to the Corning Museum of Glass, glass factories were not the most pleasant places to work in the early twentieth century. They were mostly run by unskilled workers, referred to as "boys" (even if they were adults). Most of the workers were men under the age of twenty-one. In fact, the majority of the employees were only sixteen or seventeen years old. They often worked ten hours a day, and a workweek of fifty to fifty-five hours was typical. (This was years before overtime pay!) Women were usually hired to be inspectors or packers, because they were thought to have a better "eye" for that kind of work. The average hourly pay for men was between fifteen and eighteen cents an hour. Women were paid just eleven cents.

The three most common positions were crack-off boys, lehr boys, and mold boys. Crack-off boys had the job of removing a finished piece of heated glassware from the end of an iron. As their name states, these boys would crack the piece off, often by applying a small amount of water to the top of the piece and then tapping on it so that it loosened from the iron. Lehr boys would carry the hot glassware to the lehr, or heated kiln. Mold boys sat next to the gaffers, or glassblowers, and opened and closed the mold for the glass when instructed.

Although the work conditions were hot, dirty, and often risky, glasswork was a way to make a decent income in the early twentieth century. Gaffers (glassblowers) with experience were in high demand. To get hired, a gaffer simply had to walk into the nearest saloon—a common hiring spot—and apply.

Working with glass means measuring and cutting it, following very precise measurements and using specialized sharp cutting tools.

construction workers initiative, told *U.S. News & World Report*, "[Being a glazier] is a physical job as compared to most." It often involves quite a bit of bending, lifting, stretching, kneeling, carrying, and moving around heavy materials.

Does this mean girls need not apply? Not at all. While glasswork has historically been a primarily male profession, more women are joining the trade every year. Jennifer Outland, a glazier apprentice, told the Northwestern Ohio Construction Education Center, "I was a little anxious at first because of the physical and mental demands the trade has." But she continued, "My reward for accepting the challenge is a satisfying career with high pay." In the *U.S. News* report on careers in glasswork, Renne noted that increasing numbers of women are becoming glaziers. In fact, technological advances are making it much easier for anybody interested in glasswork to find a position as a glazier, regardless of physical strength.

High school shop classes teach many of the skills that are applied in trade careers, including glasswork.

THE BRAVE WINDOW WASHERS

Glass is beautiful, but it also gets dirty. It's easy to clean a window if you just have to step outside, but what happens when dirty

Window washers can't be afraid of heights and must be willing to spend hours outside, hundreds of feet up in the air—yet still know how to avoid leaving any streaks.

windows are ten, twenty, thirty, or even one hundred stories high? That's when you call on the bravest cleaners in the world: professional window washers.

The first window washers would simply lean out through windows and grip the frame. By the early twentieth century, leather safety belts were added to hold workers in the building. In 1952, the first scaffold was built for washers to stand on.

Today, window washers rely on high-tech equipment to keep them safe hundreds of feet above the ground. For example, the team that washes the windows of the forty-five-story Hearst Tower in New York City has a high-tech scaffold referred to in a February 2013 article by the *New Yorker* as "a little monster." This rectangular steel box is the size of a small car. It contains a computer that monitors sixty-seven different safety sensors and switches to ensure they are working properly. A remote control with more than a dozen buttons controls the movement of the rig.

Cleaning the windows of any skyscraper is a slow process. It can take anywhere from one month to six months to complete cleaning from top to bottom. One of a window washer's biggest enemies is wind. It can cause water to streak and rock the scaffolding. Safety is a key component. Equipment must be checked often to be sure it is working properly.

Alcides Moreno, a New York–based window washer, can tell you about the dangers of window washing. On December 7, 2007, Moreno fell forty-seven stories when his scaffolding broke. To everyone's shock, he lived, although he had almost a dozen broken bones and needed sixteen different surgeries. However, after months of physical therapy, Moreno was able to walk again and even participated in a 5K run for charity.

Glasswork can be tough—but it is also exciting and one of the most stable trade professions in the country. It does not require a college degree but, as with most trades, focuses on a four-year apprenticeship that combines classes with on-the-job training.

What Does It Take?

Besides some strong muscles and the ability to work outside, what traits or skills do potential glassworkers need? Most apprenticeships ask for applicants to be at least eighteen years old, to have a high school diploma or GED, and to hold a valid driver's license.

In addition, a strong background in math and design are helpful, as well as any prior familiarity with construction equipment. If your school has shop classes, for example, they are a great way to introduce you to working with different materials and machines. Don't ignore those important computer skills, however. As the world of glasswork becomes more advanced, there is a growing use of computers within the business.

Other important qualities include balance, strong hand-eye coordination, and physical stamina. Steady hands and good vision are also critical traits. Glasswork often carries the risk of getting cut, and so it is essential that glassworkers follow all safety precautions and use common sense.

Being comfortable with heights is also important if you decide to get into commercial glasswork. Chances are you might be working high up in the air. You will need to focus on placing glass and not worry about heights. Most important, however, is the desire to learn and discover an exciting career. "If you have a willingness to learn and a willingness to work, and you're good at what you do," Renne said encouragingly, "you're always going to find an opportunity to work."

chapter 2

THE ART OF GLASS

What is it like to be a glazier? A glazier's day can be long, especially when a construction project has a tight timeline. Complications often come up in construction, so construction workers, including glaziers, must be prepared to work swiftly and solve problems as they come up. However, the work is very rewarding. Glaziers learn great skills that go beyond construction into computer programming and design.

In September 2006, one glazier, Alfonso Marin-Garcia, shared his experiences as a glazier in an essay for *Glass Magazine* titled "A Day in the Life of a Glass Worker." Marin-Garcia said that he must start work early, usually around 7 AM. "Every day, I learn something new at my job," he shared. He spoke about one twelve-hour day that he spent learning about a new high-tech computer system programmed to cut, polish, and fabricate sheets of glass. The system was complicated, and some of the first orders came out wrong and needed to be revised.

Marin-Garcia also recalled that when he first started, he had to be on hand to help with whatever was needed. After learning the basics, however, he "learned to operate the crane that transports sheets of glass or mirrors to the cutting table." Over time, he learned a great deal about glass and safety. "I have learned a lot about glass including the fact that you have to work very carefully with it," he said. After years on the job, Marin-Garcia still loves his job. So what are the day-to-day tasks for a glazier? Let's take a look.

Wearing protective equipment is essential in a field like glasswork. Doing the job well is important, but doing it safely is even more so.

BASIC TASKS FOR A GLAZIER

While the daily duties any glazier has will change from project to project, there are many common tasks that most glaziers must do on any given project. First, glaziers must follow blueprints or specifications for the project. This means that glaziers must know how to read blueprints just as an architect or contractor would. Blueprints can have specialized notations, so a glazier should learn how to understand them. Having a visual mind that can translate the 2D blueprint into a 3D building helps, too.

After studying the blueprint, glaziers must work in real life. Task one is often removing old or broken glass in preparation to install replacements. They also must cut glass to the determined size and shape. Any errors in the cut and the glass might not fit, so glaziers must work with precision.

After the glass is cut, glaziers must make sashes (fixed or moveable frameworks) or moldings (strips of wood to go around windows) for installing glass. They then must fasten the glass to the sashes with clips or other fasteners.

The final step is to add weather seal or putty around the edges of the glass to seal the joints.

If you are a glazier working on a commercial project with multiple stories and large pieces of glass, you will also learn how to work with cranes and hoists to move large, heavy panes of glass. Along with glass, glaziers are often also taught how to

"ONCE YOU START, YOU JUST CAN'T STOP"

One group of people who know how beautiful glass can be are the members of the Glass Art Society. Since 1971, their mission has been to "encourage excellence, to advance education, to promote the appreciation and development of the glass arts, and to support the worldwide community of artists who work with glass." For years, the society has sponsored an annual conference that brings together glass artists and experts from all over the world. Over a thousand people attend three days of lectures, panels, and demonstrations about glass each year.

The yearly conference is for anyone who loves art—or glass. Each year the conference is held in a different city. Local art galleries and museums show off their glass art exhibitions. The latest in equipment, supplies, and services are displayed, and resources about glass schools and research are offered. An international student exhibition features the original glasswork of area students.

For students who are interested in working with glass, the Glass Art Society's executive director Pamela Koss says, "There are some great high school programs to explore in glass art. Many art schools also offer a survey course in glass that lets you find out how it feels—a sampling. Many people say, especially with hot glass, that once you start, you just can't stop."

When working on multistory buildings, glaziers rely on large cranes to lift the heavy panes of glass to where the workers are waiting.

work with alternative glass materials, such as plastics, granite, and marble.

Tools of the Trade

Glaziers spend their days cutting, finishing, measuring, carrying, and installing glass. To do this, they have a unique set of tools.

While large companies often rely on high-tech computers to cut glass into specific shapes and sizes, other glassworkers use cutting wheels or glass cutters. Cutting wheels are frequently made out of steel and have a sharpened edge. They look like a pizza cutter. Oil glass cutters are almost the same, but they have a built-in reservoir for oil to keep the wheel lubricated. Circle cutters combine a cutting wheel with a suction cup and an attached arm for cutting circles and ovals. If the glazier needs a simple straight line, a strip cutter is often used.

Finishing tools are used to make the edges and surfaces of glass smooth. Sometimes, files or stones are used to smooth rough edges, but most of the time, glass grinders are used. These machines come in all sizes, from small and handheld ones to grinders that are huge and fixed in place.

Glaziers spend a lot of time measuring, too. Precise measurements are important. A glass piece that is cut the wrong length, width, or thickness is going to cause nothing but trouble when it is installed. It will either be too big, be too small, or simply not fit at all. To ensure proper measurements, glassworkers might use anything from a basic tape measure to a high-tech electronic glass-measuring tool.

It might surprise you to learn that one of the hardest parts of glasswork is learning how to carry a piece of glass properly. If you think back to the last time you saw a drinking glass shatter on the floor, however, it will become clear why this

Glaziers use cutting wheels and other glasswork tools along with high-tech computer systems to measure and cut glass perfectly.

step has to be done so carefully. Glaziers are often working with panes of glass twice their height and weighing hundreds of pounds. Just imagine what it would be like if one of those panes dropped and broke! Glaziers need the right tools to help them

A combination of belt sanders, water, and a steady hand ensure that the edges of glass plates are smooth and straight.

carry these panes of glass. One of the most common types is vacuum or suction cups. These fasten tightly to the surface of the glass. A handle makes it easier to lift, hold, and move the glass. For larger pieces, glaziers might use carrying straps. The largest pieces are often moved by a combination of cranes, hoists, and ropes. In these projects, glaziers work closely with a team of construction workers.

Installation tools vary greatly. It takes far more sophisticated equipment to install huge glass panes on the side of a high-rise than it does to put a mirror in a bathroom. The main tool used is a glazier knife, although glazier knives come in different shapes and sizes. These knives are primarily used to push putty and other fastening material into place in order to hold the glass. Lead knives, cutting pliers, and soldering irons are used when the piece of glass is being held in place by lead.

Installing glass takes more than tools. The glass has to be fastened into place. This can be done with a cement mixture called mastic, as well as putty, concrete, rivets, springs, molding, or rubber gaskets. Rubber gaskets are long rubber half-tubes that have been split down the middle. The gasket is pushed into place around the

A glazier knife is designed to push putty or other sealing agents into the edges of a glass pane in order to hold the glass in place.

frame, and then the edge of the glass is pushed into it. Some other tools commonly used by glaziers include levels, grinding and polishing machines, power saws, and lifts.

GLASS AS ART

There is no question that glaziers work on amazing projects. Take a look at some of the most beautiful glass buildings throughout the world for proof. The National Centre for the Performing Arts in Beijing, China, the Botanical Garden of Curitiba in Brazil, the Aldar headquarters building in Abu Dhabi, the Sage Gateshead in the United Kingdom, and the pyramid at the Louvre Museum in Paris, France, are all examples of extraordinary glass architecture. Each one is incredible to behold and draws tourists from near and far.

Glass is actually a wonderful medium for making all kinds of art. Glass can be engraved or etched with special tools. Glass can be combined with color to create stained glass images. It can be heated and poured into molds to create everything from sculptures to dishware. It can also be used for the centuries-old art of glassblowing.

In glassblowing, molten or liquid glass is created by heating quartz sand to very high temperatures and then adding sodium carbonate and lime. Other ingredients are added to change the color. Everything gets combined in a cauldron and then heated. The glassblower uses a long metal pipe, known as a blowpipe. The pipe is dipped into the heated mixture and turned until a ball of glass forms at the end. Then, the glassblower takes the pipe out of the fire and begins to carefully and lightly blow into it. This makes the glass stretch and form into shapes. To alter the shape, glassblowers use paddles and pinchers called calipers to press, pull, squeeze, and twist the glass into the desired shape. It might be a figurine, a vase, or a paperweight. Once the glass is done, it is left to cool.

The China National Grand Theatre in Beijing shows what incredible effects glass can have when shaped and polished.

A Career Cutting Glass

Working as a glazier or a glassblower aren't the only careers for somebody passionate about glass. Glass cutting can also be a profitable career option for the artistic person who wants to cut designs into glass to sell commercially. When Gary Eshleman first saw someone crafting cut glass, he described it as "fascinating, almost intoxicating." He wanted to learn how to do it, and over time, Eshleman learned how to cut designs onto glass vases, glasses, paperweights, bowls, plates, and thin glass holiday decorations. "The thing I liked best about cutting glass," he explained in an e-mail interview, "was designing patterns and reproducing those patterns in the style that I had imagined in my head. This kind of cut glass is done freehand, for the most part, so you cannot make any mistakes." In 1999, Eshleman opened his own glassware store, called Crystal Shadows, in Goshen, Indiana. He sells his glass creations.

The skills required for cutting designs into glass, according to Eshleman, are pretty straightforward. "You need steady hands, and to get steady hands, you have to practice," he stated. "The steady hand helps you translate a pattern onto glass." In addition to steady hands, he recommended that students have basic mechanical skills so they can learn to set and sharpen the wheels. "You also need to have some artistic design skills—a sense of balance and symmetry," he added. Eshleman also suggested that anyone interested in artistic glass cutting should be able to work long hours and pay great attention to detail.

When it comes to what equipment to use, Eshleman said he chooses what kinds of wheels to use and how to sharpen them. "When you are cutting," he described, "the wheel particulates and the glass particulates must be swept from the wheel. This is done with a wet sponge in contact with the wheel. Too much wetness obscures your view of the glass," he continued. "Too little and the glass will burn and you will end up breathing the particulates into your lungs."

Eshleman's advice to young people who might want to learn to cut glass is encouraging. "Do not listen to people who say you cannot do this...One of the best things in the world is earning money doing what you like." Glassblowing and glass cutting are two artistic careers in glasswork that may be more fulfilling than work as a glazier.

Whether it's being used to build secure windows and storefronts or shaped into delicate flower vases, glass is an incredible medium. Becoming a glazier or glassworker takes years, but the hard work is worth it. It shows you how to take glass and use it to create buildings and please the senses.

chapter 3

Earn While You Learn with an Apprenticeship

What comes to mind when you hear the term "trade career"? If you're like many people, you may think that trade careers are only for people who cannot go to college because of poor grades or cost. However, trade careers are a tremendous choice for students. Just ask Mike Rowe, the host of Discovery Channel's *Dirty Jobs* and CNN's *Somebody's Gotta Do It*. Rowe is the founder of the mikeroweWORKS Foundation and Profoundly Disconnected. These organizations are dedicated to giving scholarships to students who are pursuing a career in the skilled trades.

In 2011, Rowe testified before the U.S. Senate on the importance of trade careers and the skilled labor shortage in the United States. He said the problem was due to a misperception about trade careers. Rowe said:

> **In high schools, the vocational arts have all but vanished. We've elevated the importance of higher education to such a lofty perch that all other forms of knowledge are now labeled alternative. Millions of parents and kids see apprenticeships and on-the-job training opportunities as vocational consolation prizes, best suited for those not cut out for a four-year degree.**

Rowe's organizations are working to try and correct popular misunderstandings about trade careers such as careers as a glazier. He hopes that these groups, along with his testimony, will help close the "skills gap," or the mismatch between the kinds of

Mike Rowe emphasizes the importance of trade careers. His organizations and television shows highlight the importance of fields such as glasswork.

skills employers are looking for and the kinds of skills the workforce actually has. Rowe continued, "Closing the skills gap doesn't just benefit future tradesmen and the companies desperate to hire them. It benefits people like me, and anyone else who shares my addiction to paved roads, reliable bridges, heating, air conditioning, and indoor plumbing."

Just as Rowe told the Senate, trade careers are a wonderful option for many young people. Job opportunities in trade careers are growing daily, and so is the average pay rate for these types of jobs. Glasswork is one of the trades that require an apprenticeship, which allows students to learn while on the job. It can be done immediately after high school graduation as well.

THE APPRENTICESHIP

Most glassworkers take a three- or four-year apprenticeship as training before working on their own as a glazier. Each one of those years typically consists of 144 hours of technical training and 2,000 hours of paid, on-the-job training. Apprenticeships are offered through unions, contractor associations, and technical and community colleges. Classes vary a bit from one school or union to another, but many courses

Glasswork has been an art form for centuries. This glass quartz ceramic jar from Babylon dates to the eleventh or twelfth century BCE.

are standard across the board.

First, an important course for any prospective construction worker is one in standard workplace safety. Such classes usually cover climbing, lifting, rigging, and hoisting; hazardous materials and fire protection; and the use of scaffolding and access equipment, as well as the use of swing stage scaffolding. While learning these basic safety rules can feel like a chore, the

The Cutting Edge

Working with glass, according to Matthew Arrigale, vice president of human resources for major glass manufacturer SCHOTT North America, gives young people the chance to work on the cutting edge of an age-old material. "It allows them to take a material that has been around for thousands of years, and then foster its continuous development," he explained in an e-mail interview. "Glass is a material that touches every person, every day, whether we notice it or not," he continued. "Glass is a material with great potential, so the applications for the end product are endless. It is a great career for people with curious minds. Specifically, [it is for] individuals who are constantly seeking new ways to solve problems and thrive on innovation."

SCHOTT is a leading international technology group in the areas of specialty glass and glass ceramics. The company employs more than 15,000 people worldwide, 2,200 of whom are in North America. Arrigale said that students who might want to become glassworkers need a few key qualifications. "An interest in math and science is obviously very important, since glasswork is a very technical profession," he stated, "but soft skills are also highly valued. Applicants need to be able to communicate effectively, work as a team, and show a high level of creativity. Cross-cultural skills are vital also, as all types of people work in the glasswork profession."

importance of safety at a construction site (especially for glaziers, who will be working with heavy glass and potentially dangerous equipment) is essential.

A course in basic construction tools is also common for most careers in the field. This type of class will cover the use of hand tools, portable and stationary power tools, and fasteners, adhesives, and sealants.

For an apprenticeship in glasswork, there will be specialized classes on glass to supplement general courses on construction tools and safety. These classes will cover types of glass, the storage and handling of glass, glass manufacturing, glass cutting and edging, and sandblasting and etching. This will, of course, be accompanied by a course on glazing tools. Learning about glazing tools will prepare a glazier-to-be for work on window systems, auto glass, flat glass, residential and commercial glazing, structural glazing, and specialty glazing. Furthermore, this class is where a prospective glazier will learn industry codes and standards. Advanced courses will also teach a glazier-to-be more advanced glasswork, such as sloped glazing (think of glass roofs or the glass on skyscrapers) and skylights.

You might expect that being a glazier is all about physical strength, but a strong background in math and computer sciences is also needed. That's because glaziers must often calculate precise measurements, and the industry is increasingly using high-tech software to do these calculations. Courses in math and drawing interpretation will teach an apprentice math fundamentals such as ratio, proportion, and percentage. They'll also cover glasswork-specific applications of math, such as glazing material calculations, and various types of drawing. The majority of programs also include some courses on different levels of welding and basic blueprint reading.

Apprentices spend at least one day a week in the classroom, but they spend far more time on the job learning skills and putting their studies to practice. While they are at work, they are earning

It's All in the Attitude

After being a glazier journeyman for more than twenty-nine years and instructor for fifteen, Alan Brown knew what to look for in future glaziers. As the first full-time training coordinator for the glazier apprenticeship program at Oregon's Mt. Hood Community College, Brown said successful apprentices boil down to one thing: attitude. "It is the main thing," he said in a June 2015 phone interview. "If a person has a good attitude, you can teach him anything." Another helpful trait to have is dependability. "Get to work on time," he said. "Otherwise, it is the best way to lose your job." He looks for young people who are able to "put down their cell phones for eight hours a day." He struggles the most with young people who have not yet learned these important lessons.

MHCC's apprenticeship program lasts for four years. Students have 8,000 hours worth of on-the-job training and 144 hours per year of college courses. They go to school one night a week for four years and spend the rest of the time on job sites. They are paid for their time on the job and get pay increases every one thousand hours. "The first year is all about basics," described Brown. "We teach students how to pick up and carry a piece of glass, as well as get it out of the case for cutting. They learn how to cut, notch, drill and polish the edges, plus take an OSHA safety course." The second year focuses on blueprint reading and advanced safety classes. This is the year students get many of their certifications. The third year centers on welding. "They practice, practice, practice welding," said Brown. The fourth year is all about technical layouts for high-rise buildings and specialty classes. In addition, students build projects and have them put into a test chamber that simulates a hurricane to see if the projects can endure.

"Glasswork is heavy, hard work," said Brown, but it is also incredibly rewarding. "At the end of the day, you can see what you have accomplished," he stated with pride. "Every night, when I turn on the news, I see something I've done."

With an apprenticeship in glasswork, apprentices can learn directly from veteran glaziers, both in the classroom and on the job site.

a wage. Usually, in the first year, this pay is about 45 percent of what a full glazier journeyman or journeywoman earns. Generally, this rate is increased for every one thousand hours the student earns, about six months of classes. By the time the apprenticeship is complete, the student is earning almost 100 percent of what a full journeyman or journeywoman is paid.

BY THE NUMBERS

After an apprenticeship is finished, the journeyman or journeywoman glazier earns a full wage. For the most recent statistics on glazier wages in the United States, consult the Bureau of Labor Statistics' (BLS) *Occupational Outlook Handbook*. There you can find the average yearly income for a glazier as well as the range of pay rates for any given year. Pay can vary widely, so it's good to know that glaziers who are members of a union usually have higher incomes than those who are not part of a union. In a 2012 report, the BLS predicted that glazier employment would grow 17 percent in the decade between then and 2022, especially in the southern United States and in the United States' largest cities. That growth rate was higher than the average across all job fields at the time of the report.

An apprenticeship has many advantages to it. Instead of paying money to learn, apprentices earn money while they learn. They graduate without the typically huge debt from student loans, bank loans, or tuition fees that most students face. When they finish, most apprentices go directly into full-time jobs in their chosen field. They have spent those years meeting the people and resources they need to find employment. As Mike Rowe stated, trade careers are one of the best choices young people can make today. They are a way to learn, earn, and join the workforce effectively and efficiently.

chapter 4

Advanced Licensing for Glaziers

At last, the apprenticeship is over. But does that mean, as a journeyman or journeywoman, that you're done learning? Definitely not. One of the biggest advantages to trade careers is that the chance to keep improving, take new classes, and keep discovering new techniques, ideas, and methods is always there. Why stop at being a glazier? What else can you do that will not only make you more employable but also earn a higher wage?

After a glazier apprentice earns the title of journeyman or journeywoman and has been working for a year, he or she is classified as a Level I glazier. With additional training and years on the job, a person can rise to Level II. This involves additional training in the glasswork for storefronts, curtain walls, and commercial interior and residential projects. For those who want to be experts at glasswork, there is another level, a Level III glazier (also referred to as a "master glazier"). The National Glass Association offers written examinations that certify a glazier's competency level.

Large storefront windows are a specialty in glasswork. A number of stores depend heavily on these windows to display their products.

SAMPLE QUESTIONS FROM THE GLAZIER EXAM

Preparing for your glazier exam is easier if you know what type of questions to expect. Here are a few examples from the Industry Training Authority's Glazier Exam:

Glass in slope glazing has broken during a snowstorm and a rafter appears to have sagged. What is the first step before reglazing?

Remove the broken glass.
Remove the snow from the skylight.
Secure the skylight from underneath.
Take measurements for the replacement glass.

How is the crate positioned when crating [packing] glass before shipping?

Flat on the floor
Perpendicular to the floor
Slipped over stacked glass
Leaning at 15 degrees against a solid support

What is done before handling hazardous material required for glass installation?

Check the WHMIS label
Check the packing slip
Check with the foreman
Wear protective clothing

Taking online practice tests will give you an idea of the types of challenges that glaziers face on the job. Just like with any standardized tests, practice exams are the best preparation for the real deal.

And the more practice tests you take, the better your shots are of passing the real exam! Take note of which questions you get wrong and brush up on those lessons in glasswork. These test-taking skills will help you do well at all sorts of tests in school and exams for trade certifications.

BECOMING A MASTER GLAZIER

How does a journeyman or journeywoman become a master glazier? Typically, schools require a person to have at least five years of experience before he or she can enroll in courses to become a Level III, or master, glazier. Then, the glazier must pass seven of the nine required courses to earn the certification. The nine courses are:

- Structural Glazing
- Specialty Glass
- Blueprint Reading
- Surveying for Glaziers
- Air Seal Barrier
- Project and Site Management
- Craftsmanship
- Supervision and Mentoring
- Doors and Related Hardware

After each level of training, glaziers take an exam. These exams last ninety minutes and contain all multiple-choice questions. They are taken on a computer. Recertification is required every three years to ensure that glaziers know the latest safety and equipment standards in use.

In addition to earning a higher-level education, glaziers can also move into work as glazing supervisors, general construction supervisors, independent contractors, or cost estimators. All these important jobs oversee the work of glaziers and other construction workers on major projects. And the greater the responsibility, the better the payday!

The National Glass Association's career training programs also include training to become a certified auto glass technician, a certified architectural glass technician, or a certified window and door installer. These classes are taken online, but they include a forty-hour internship and a training manual. Two years after initially offering these courses, the NGA announced that more than two thousand auto glass technicians had earned their certifications. "This is indeed a wonderful achievement," stated Steve Mort, chairman of the board of directors of the NGA, in a press release.

BECOMING A GLASS SPECIALIST

While virtually all glaziers measure, cut, prepare, and install glass, some decide to pursue a specialty within the field. For example, a glass-worker might specialize in

Understanding the unique symbols and coding in blueprints is a skill all glassworkers need. These roadmaps tell glaziers exactly where the glass will go in a new building.

Breaking Glass for a Living

Have you ever dropped your cell phone or tablet? For most light falls, the glass doesn't break. You may not have realized it, but the hardened glass on the front of your devices is called Gorilla Glass. It is found in more than 2.7 billion electronic devices. Gorilla Glass

The Gorilla Glass used in electronics such as most cell phones is resilient and durable. It can often withstand small falls without cracking.

is a product of Corning. Since 2007, it has been used to protect each generation of cell phones, laptops, smartwatches, and tablets from the cracks associated with minor falls. While it does scratch, Gorilla Glass has become increasingly difficult to break over the years. To make sure the glass works—and to make improvements—engineers at Corning spend their day dropping, bending, shattering, puncturing, and scratching the glass. "We primarily break glass. It's our job," said Corning technology manager Jon Pesansky in an October 2014 interview with CNET.

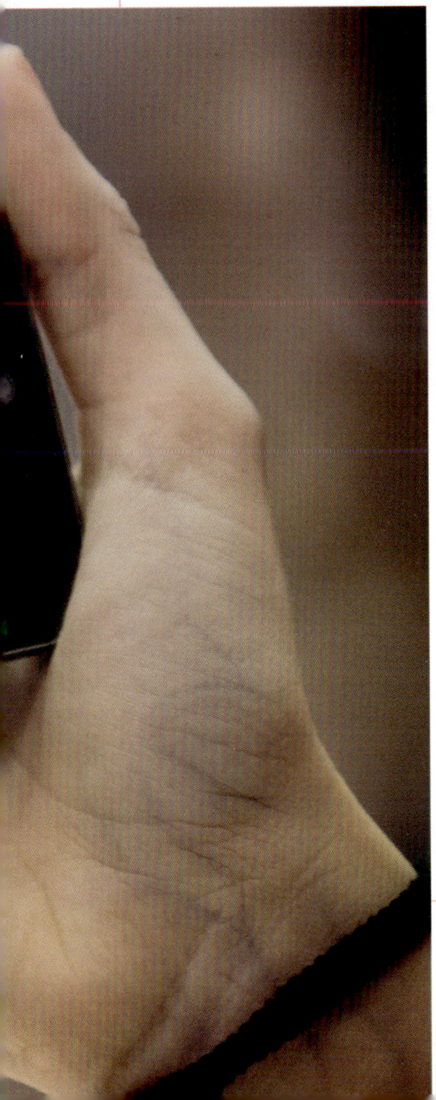

At Corning, lab engineers use machines to drop metal balls on the glass from different heights to see what it takes to crack the glass. Corning scientist Kevin Reiman said, "Part of what we're doing is looking at the real details of how things break in the field and then bringing that back into the laboratory to generate new tests, so we can evaluate the damage resistance of glass better, so we can design better glass."

Reiman's job is to study the cracks in the glass—a field called fractography—when it does break and figure out how it happened. "It's like detective work, looking for clues, looking for evidence, piecing it together and putting the story together," Reiman told CNET. "It's a lot like [the crime detective television show] *CSI*, in a way, because you're letting the glass tell the story of how did it break." In addition to making stronger glass, Corning hopes to make glass that reflects less light, repels water, and resists oil.

becoming a glass silverer, a leadlight worker, a furniture or millworking glassworker, or a glass beveller.

GLASS SILVERERS

Have you ever wondered what turns a piece of simple glass into a mirror? This is the job of a glass silverer. First, the glassworker chooses the right piece of glass and polishes it. Next, he or she sprays a silvering solution over the surface of the glass. The silverer may add more than one layer. Finally, the mirror is washed and dried, and a special coating is applied to it. Now it is ready to be framed and hung.

LEADLIGHT WORKERS

A leadlight worker tends to work with stained glass windows (such as the ones commonly seen in churches), doors, partitions, and other decorative pieces. The pieces of different colored glass are fit together with strips of lead. They are often held in place with putty.

Stained glass lends a beautiful and colorful slant to any project, whether in a sanctuary or in a home or office.

MILLWORKING GLASSWORKERS

A furniture or millworking glassworker installs glass into premade pieces of wood and metal products, including doors, window sashes, partitions, and cabinets. This work might entail building a table or a coffee table with a glass top or glasswork in cabinetry.

GLASS BEVELLERS

A glass beveller has the job of making glass more beautiful. He or she does this by beveling, or smoothing, the edges of flat glass items such as mirrors or tabletops. This makes the edges safer and more attractive. To create smooth edges, a glass beveller uses grinding wheels or abrasive belts. Depending on the project, he or she might also drill a hole or put notches on the ends of the glass.

THE RISE OF DECORATIVE GLASS

Many specialty jobs in glasswork are becoming more important since a growing number of people are interested in adding decorative glass—that is, glass that serves for beauty rather than function—to their homes and businesses. In a March 2014 article, Chris Mammen, president of M3 Glass Technologies told *Glass Magazine*, "The decorative glass market is changing so fast. Things that were new, unique, or special just a couple of years ago are now old-hat and more common. Everybody, from designers to building owners, from glass fabricators to equipment manufacturers, is constantly looking to do something new with decorative glass." Of course, this means glaziers need to learn new techniques and skills in order to keep up.

One of the biggest demands in decorative glass today is for vibrantly colored glass. No more plain, translucent glass—but bright shades of red, blue, purple, yellow, and every other tint you can imagine. Another trend is textured glass, including glass with zigzags, circles, and ripples etched into it. Digitally printed glass—or glass with images printed on it—is also becoming far more popular, as is laminated glass, or glass that has been made to look like fabric, mesh, or other designs. Glass floors, along with huge glass panels are gaining popularity as well. This is because glass is beautiful, and as new technology makes glass a more feasible option, people are demanding it to make their residential and commercial buildings brighter, sleeker, and more open.

Going Green

Have you heard people talking about "going green" or "leaving a smaller carbon footprint"? These phrases refer to the global movement toward protecting the earth from damage and not using up its limited natural resources. A number of construction projects today are built with these ideas in mind. Glassworkers who know how to use glass in an energy-efficient manner have a long and profitable future ahead of them. Using glass in a "green" manner means knowing how to let the right amount of sunlight in while still managing glare and reducing solar heat gain (the increase in temperature created by that sunshine).

Windows provide insulation to buildings, preventing the loss of air conditioning in the summer and the loss of heat in the winter. Double-paned windows—or windows with two panes of glass and a built-in space between them—lose less cool air (in the summer) and heat (in the winter). This makes them a great—and green—choice! Also key to good insulation is tightly sealed windows.

To make sure they understand how to use glass in an environmentally friendly way, some glaziers pursue additional

Replacing traditional windows with double-glazed windows helps reduce the need for heating and cooling inside a home. It saves homeowners money and helps protect the environment.

education and certification from companies such as the Green Advantage or Leadership in Energy and Environmental Design (LEED). This type of certification will pay off when new projects with a green focus seek out the most qualified glaziers for their needs. Better insulation also saves money on air conditioning and heat, meaning "green" windows pay for themselves in savings on the electricity bill.

Like every profession, the field of glasswork is constantly changing. What people want out of their homes and businesses changes with time. So do the types of tools and technologies that are available for glaziers. Likewise, the training and education available for journeymen and journeywomen changes. The successful glazier keeps track of these new tools and technologies and makes sure to adapt to them.

chapter 5

Hitting the Job Market

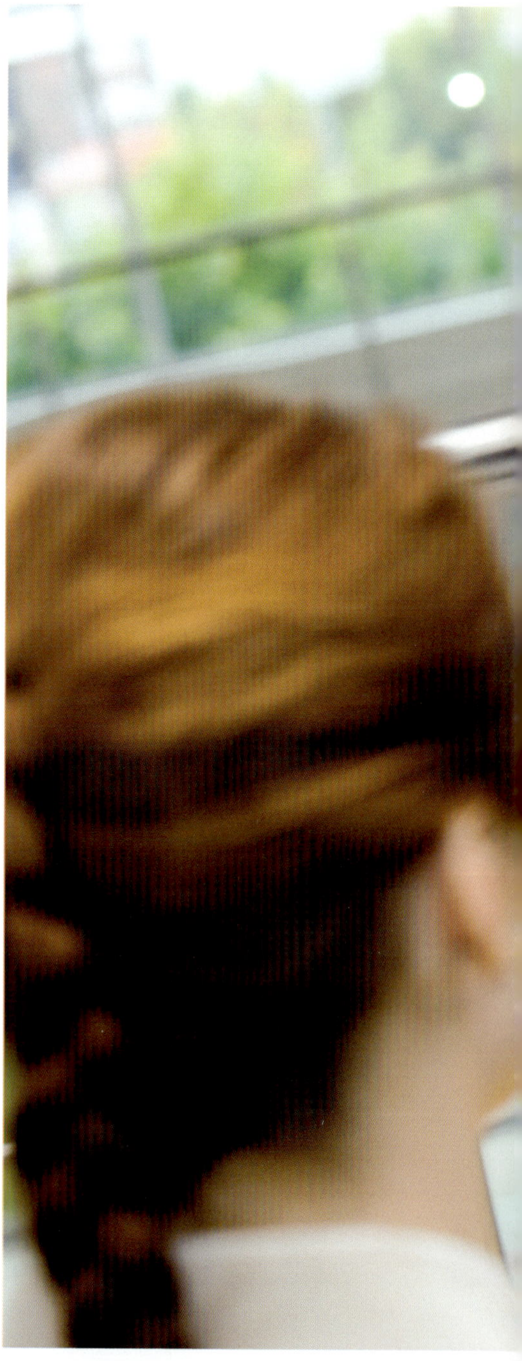

Looking for a job, regardless of the field, can be overwhelming. The idea of going from one company to the next selling your experience and skills can be intimidating. In trade careers, however, there is one major advantage. After several years of working on different job sites as apprentices, journeymen and journeywomen glaziers typically have a long list of names and companies to get in touch with when they start looking for a full-time job. If a glassworker has spent those years networking, talking, and reaching out to coworkers and bosses, it will be fairly easy for him or her to figure out where to start putting in those applications. This is especially true if he or she joins a glassworkers union.

The process of applying for a job as a glassworker is much the same as any other field. Candidates need a strong cover letter and résumé to start with. They also need to prepare for one-on-one

*Even for a **trade** career, presenting a professional image during your interview is important.*

THE RIGHT QUESTIONS AND ANSWERS

While nothing can guarantee you a job offer after an interview, there are some ways to increase your chances. One is knowing what questions to ask and which ones to avoid. A March 2014 article in *Fortune Magazine* listed the worst questions asked by job applicants. They included, "How soon can I take my first vacation?" and, "Is the boss single?" Oftentimes, trade careers involve working in laid-back environments. However, professionalism—especially in the job interview—is important.

Are there questions you should ask? In a February 2013 article in *Glass Magazine*, Michelle Messersmith, manager of employee services at Walters & Wolf, spoke about her company's hiring practices. She said, "Unfortunately, there is no one magic question that will tell us if we found the perfect candidate. It takes a good understanding of what the job requires, well formulated questions, and lots of practice." She shared that at Walters & Wolf, they use an interview technique called behavioral interviewing. "This type of interview can determine how a person will act or think in the future if a similar scenario presents itself," she explained. "For example, 'Give me a specific example of a time when you improved a function or process that you knew you could make better.'"

Bob Garner, vice president of human resources at Lee & Cates Glass, thinks an interview should focus on an applicant's track record on the job. "So among many questions, the most important question that I ask is, 'What is your greatest achievement and worst failure in your past job?'" he told *Glass Magazine*. "What I am looking for is the following: Do they admit to any? Do they blame others? Is the candidate self-assured? Have they learned from mistakes and, if so, what did they learn?" You don't need to hide or cover up your areas of improvement in a job interview.

Be honest, and let a potential employer know you are ready and excited to improve on your existing skill set in your new position.

Support your résumé with a cover letter, and remember that first impressions can never be changed, so remain professional at all times.

can use this time well. After all, if you are called in for an in-person interview, you'll need to know what questions you'll be asked by the employer—and which ones to ask back, as well.

Adding windows or glass to a new building can change its feel. Glaziers help people let the sunshine in, keep the rain out, and enjoy the view.

Interviews can make or break getting a job offer, and so answering questions well and asking intelligent questions is vital. To prepare for a face-to-face interview, people often make a list of questions and then practice their answers until they have memorized them and can respond without hesitation. While trade careers—and the interviews for a position in one—often occur in unconventional or laid-back settings, professionalism is still important. Wear business attire to your job interview. Nice posture—for example, a firm handshake, solid eye contact, and sitting up straight—will also project the appearance of a professional employee.

Occasionally, a glazier will be offered a job right at the end of an interview. Most of the time, however, that's not the case. Most companies conduct a number of interviews with several different candidates. They will make their final choice only after they have had a chance to meet every applicant. It can be hard to be patient, but it pays off. Whether or not a glazier gets the job, it is always a good idea to send a quick thank-you e-mail or note to the person who conducted your interview. It shows maturity and gratitude—and it might just

You Never Know What to Expect

Carefully, Gunther Paulus removes a molten mass from a gas oven and pours it into a mold. It is a dangerous move—and one that takes a steady hand and a lot of experience. The liquid mass is an unbelievable 2,948 degrees Fahrenheit (1,620 degrees Celsius), so a second person is required to protect Paulus. The second worker holds a metal plate on the inside of the open oven door to shield Paulus from the most intense heat.

Paulus has been a development engineer in laboratory melting at SCHOTT since 1987. He works at their Mainz, Germany, branch. He is responsible for testing various types of glass manufacturing techniques, plus identifying the right type of melting process to use on different materials.

Because Paulus works with such high temperatures, he wears a two-layered heat protective suit, a protective hood with Plexiglass, dark glasses to protect his eyes from embers, and safety gloves. He works with gas furnaces and rotary kilns. Paulus chooses what types of chemicals to use when mixing special glass, as some types can use as many as twenty different chemical elements.

What is the best part of Paulus's job in glasswork? In his own words, "The unique thing about my job is the variety—You really never know what to expect when you come in to work in the morning."

remind that person of a particular standout candidate. Courtesy goes a long way in the job hunt.

Glass has been a part of our lives for millennia. It dates all the way back to 3,500 BCE in ancient Mesopotamia. Today, with each passing generation, glass is used in more and more ways and plays an increasing role in architectural structure and design. Glass keeps people safe and comfortable. It makes the world a more beautiful place, and it changes shapes and color at the hands of different artists.

Perhaps one day you, too, will be a professional glassworker. As a glazier, you might work in someone's home or backyard. You might install a store's front display window or an office's inner partitions. You might even work several stories up in the air in a high-rise office building or in a luxury condominium. You might install a small piece of decorative glass in a homeowner's front door or a ten-foot high, 400-pound (180-kilogram) pane of glass with a hoist and crane.

Being a glazier is exciting work because it changes every day. It does not require an expensive college degree or leave glaziers-to-be in debt. It teaches skills that can be expanded over time and applied to other careers. National labor experts routinely project that job openings for glaziers and other trade careers will continue to grow faster than many other professions in years to come.

When *U.S. News & World Report* listed glaziers as one of the nation's best professions in 2013, it described the field of glasswork as the point "where construction meets art." The article stated that the job's ranking was based on "ample employment opportunities, competitive salaries, job security, and a manageable work-life balance." Look all around you. Glass is everywhere. Now that's job security!

glossary

bevel To smooth out, usually with a grinder.
blueprint Building plans drawn in white lines on a blue background.
candidate A person who is selected by others for a particular role.
ember A small piece of wood or other material that is on fire or heated.
etch To cut a design into something with a wheel, knife, or acid.
exhibition A display, often of art or antiques.
fabricate To make or create something.
fractography The study of how glass cracks.
freehand Drawn or created without a pattern.
gaffer The nickname for a glassblower.
hoist To raise or lift, usually by a machine.
insulation Material, such as glass, used to protect an area from sound or temperature.
journeyman/journeywoman An apprentice who has completed his or her apprenticeship.
laminate To cover something with a thin layer.
lehr A heated kiln or oven for using with glass.
mastic A cement mixture used to fasten glass into place.
molding A strip of wood that is used around windows to frame them.
notch An angular shape cut into a surface.
particulate A substance made up of tiny particles.
partition Something that separates or divides something else.
putty A soft sealing agent.
reservoir A place where water or oil is collected.

rubber gaskets Long half-tubes made of rubber and split down the middle.
sashes Fixed or moveable frameworks.
scaffolding A temporary structure put up next to a building, usually made of wood and metal, for the purpose of letting workers build.
stamina A person's ability not to collapse under stress or strain.
symmetry The correct proportions or position.
trident A three-pronged building column.

for more information

American Cut Glass Association (ACGA)
P.O. Box 482
Ramona, CA 92065
(760) 789-2715
Website: http://www.cutglass.org
Founded in 1978, the ACGA is a nonprofit organization dedicated to the study of cut glass—glass that has been entirely cut by hand with a rotating wheel. It boasts more than 1,700 members who are passionate about identifying and collecting cut glass, especially from the so-called Brilliant Period of cut glass (1876–1914).

Architectural Glass & Metal Contractors Association (AGMCA)
619 Liverpool Road
Pickering, ON L1W 1R1
Canada
(905) 420-7272
Website: http://www.agmca.ca
Established in 1979, the AGMCA is the premier organization representing unionized glaziers and glassworkers throughout Canada, protecting and advancing the interests of members of this trade career.

Art Alliance for Contemporary Glass
11700 Preston Road, Suite 660 #327
Dallas, TX 75230
(214) 890-0028
Website: http://contempglass.org
This website links to dozens of other glass organizations

and focuses on information and resources for people who collect different types of contemporary glass.

GANA: Glass Association of North America
800 SW Jackson Street, Suite 1500
Topeka, KS 66612-1200
(785) 271-0208
Website: http://www.glasswebsite.com
GANA's mission is to provide industry leadership and guidance, education, and knowledge to glaziers. The website connects readers to everything from jobs to videos about making different types of glass.

Glass Art Society
6512 23rd Avenue NW, Suite 329
Seattle, WA 98117
(206) 382-1305
Website: http://www.glassart.org
This organization is dedicated to helping and educating glass artists of all kinds. Its website provides details about its upcoming conferences and membership.

Industry Training Authority (ITA)
8100 Granville Avenue, 8th Floor
Richmond, BC V6Y 3T6
Canada
(778) 328-8700
Website: http://www.itabc.ca
The ITA is in charge of working with employers, employees, industry, labor, training providers, and governments to issue credentials, manage apprenticeships, set program standards, and increase opportunities in the trade. It provides an overview of multiple trade careers, including glaziers.

International Union of Painters and Allied Trades (IUPAT)
7234 Parkway Drive
Hanover, MD 21076
(410) 564-5900
Website: http://www.iupat.org
The IUPAT represents all kinds of trades, including glasswork. The site gives information on the apprenticeship offered by the organization.

National Glass Association
1945 Old Gallows Road, Suite 750
Vienna, VA 22182
(703) 442-4890
Website: http://www.glass.org
The NGA is the largest trade association in the United States. It offers publications, training programs, and events in the world of glass. It links to its two magazines, which can be accessed online.

Ontario Glass & Metal Association (OGMA)
1011 Upper Middle Road East, Suite 1210
Oakville, ON L6H 5Z9
Canada
(905) 827-2951
Website: http://www.ogma.ca
The OGMA promotes and protects the interests of glaziers and metalworkers in the province of Ontario. It is affiliated with other glassworkers associations throughout Canada.

Provincial Glaziers Association of Alberta (PGAA)
c/o Red Deer Construction Association
Bay #3, 7471 Edgar Industrial Bend

Red Deer, AB T4P 3Z5
Canada
Website: http://www.pgaa.ca
The PGAA ensures safety, technological advances, and general excellence in the glasswork industry in Alberta, Canada. It is affiliated with other glassworkers associations throughout Canada.

Saskatchewan Apprenticeship and Trade Certification Commission
2140 Hamilton Street
Regina, SK S4P 2E3
Canada
(877) 363-0536
Website: www.saskapprenticeship.ca
This government organization provides resources for finding apprentices in various trades and offers news, application and exam forms, and coordination of technical training.

Websites

Because of the changing nature of Internet links, Rosen Publishing has developed an online list of websites related to the subject of this book. This site is updated regularly. Please use this link to access the list:

http://www.rosenlinks.com/ECAR/Glass

for further reading

Blaxland, Wendy. *Bottles and Jars* (How Are They Made?). Salt Lake City, UT: Benchmark Books, 2010.

Christen, Carol. *What Color Is Your Parachute for Teens.* New York, NY: Ten Speed Press, 2015.

Flannagan, J. S., and H. L. Newton. *The Magnificent Magnifying Lens.* Mustang, OK: Tate Publishing, 2012.

Hayes, Amy. *Turning Sand into Glass* (Step-by-Step Transformations). New York, NY: Cavendish Square Publishing, 2015.

Koscienlniak, Bruce. *Looking at Glass Through the Ages.* Boston, MA: HMH Books for Young Readers, 2006.

La Bella, Laura. *Internship and Volunteer Opportunities for People Who Love to Build Things.* New York, NY: Rosen Publishing 2012.

Langley, Andrew. *Glass* (Everyday Materials). New York, NY: Crabtree Publishing Co., 2008.

Lassieur, Allison. *Building the Empire State Building.* North Mankato, MN: Capstone Press, 2014.

Malam, John. *You Wouldn't Want to Be a Skyscraper Builder!* (A Hazardous Job You'd Rather Not Take). London, England: Franklin Watts, 2009.

Matias, Linda. *201 Knockout Answers to Tough Interview Questions.* New York, NY: Amacom, 2009.

Mayer, Cassie. *Glass* (Materials). Portsmouth, NH: Heinemann, 2008.

Morris, Neil. *Glass* (Material that Matter). North Mankato, MN: Amicus, 2010.

Pasternak, Ceel. *Cool Careers for Girls in Construction.* Atascadero, CA: Impact Publishers, 2000.

Priwer, Shana, and Cynthia Phillips. *Skyscrapers and High Rises* (Frameworks). New York, NY: Routledge, 2014.

Scheunemann, Pam. *Cool Glass and Ceramic Projects: Creative Ways to Upcycle Your Trash into Treasure.* Edina, MN: Checkerboard Library, 2012.

Somerville, Barbara. *The Story Behind Glass* (True Stories). Portsmouth, NH: Heinemann, 2011.

Spielman, Madison. *All About Hand-Blown Glass.* Huntington Beach, CA: Teacher Created Materials, 2008.

Stewart, Melissa. *How Does Sand Become Glass* (How Does It Happen?). Basingstoke, Hampshire, England: Raintree, 2009.

Williams, Brian. *The Science of a Pair of Glasses.* Milwaukee, WI: Gareth Stevens, 2009.

bibliography

Arrigale, Matthew. Personal interview by the author. June 18, 2015.

Brown, Alan. Personal interview by the author. June 23, 2015.

Bureau of Labor Statistics, U.S. Department of Labor. *Occupational Outlook Handbook, 2014-15 Edition.* Retrieved May 22, 2015 (http://www.bls.gov/ooh/construction-and-extraction/glaziers.htm).

Corning Museum of Glass. "Jobs in a 19th-Century Glass Factory." Corning. Retrieved June 21, 2015 (http://www.cmog.org/article/jobs-19th-century-glass-factory).

Devlin, Katy. "Cladding an Icon." *Glass Magazine*, August 22, 2013. Retrieved June 14, 2015 (http://glassmagazine.com/article/commercial/cladding-icon-1311598).

Devlin, Katy. "Window to the Future of Decorative Glass." *Glass Magazine*, March 28, 2014. Retrieved June 23, 2015 (http://glassmagazine.com/article/commercial/window-future-decorative-glass-1412340).

Discovery Channel. "Mike Rowe Senate Testimony Dirty Jobs." May 11, 2011. Retrieved June 21, 2015 (http://www.discovery.com/tv-shows/dirty-jobs/lists/mike-rowe-senate-testimony).

Edelman, Susan. "He Survived 47-floor Plunge—and Now Walks for Charity." *New York Post*, January 5, 2014. Retrieved June 13, 2015 (http://nypost.com/2014/01/05/window-washer-survived-47-story-plunge-now-walks-for-charity).

Eshleman, Gary. Personal interview by the author. June 21, 2015.

Gailioto, Kristin. "Glass Art Society Invites Public to Attend Exciting Glass Events in San Jose." Glass Art Society. Retrieved June 22, 2015 (http://www.glassart.org/_Library/Press_Releases/2015_Open_to_the_Public_Press_Release.pdf).

Glass Magazine. "What Is the Most Important Question You Ask a Potential Hire? Why?" February 27, 2013. Retrieved June 15, 2015 (http://glassmagazine.com/article/commercial/g3-industry-insiders-talk-glass-1310858).

Glass Magazine. "The Worst Job Interview Questions." March 26, 2013. Retrieved June 15, 2015 (http://glassmagazine.com/article/commercial/worst-job-interview-questions-1310951).

Higginbotham, Ada. "Life at the Top." *New Yorker*, February 4, 2013. Retrieved June 22, 2015 (http://www.newyorker.com/magazine/2013/02/04/life-at-the-top).

Industry Training Authority. "Sample Test Questions Glazer." Retrieved June 22, 2015 (http://www.itabc.ca/sites/default/files/docs/manage/glazier-practice-exam.pdf).

Koss, Pamela. Personal interview by the author. June 21, 2015.

Marin-Garcia, Alfonso. "A Day in the Life of a Glassworker." *Glass Magazine*, September 1, 2006. Retrieved June 21, 2015 (http://glassmagazine.com/article/commercial/a-day-life-a-glass-worker).

Northwestern Ohio Construction Education Center. "A Day in the Life of a Glazier." NOCEC. Retrieved June 21, 2015 (http://www.nocec.com/dilo_glazier.php).

Rodriguez, Miguel. "NGA Certifications Cross Major Milestone." National Glass Association. July 14, 2009. Retrieved June 22, 2015 (https://www.glass.org/press/071409-2k_certs.htm).

Rubin, Ben Fox. "For Gorilla Glass Testers, Life Is a Daily Grind (and Scratch and Drop…). C/Net. October 29,

2014. Retrieved June 14, 2015 (http://www.cnet.com/news/for-gorilla-glass-testers-life-is-a-daily-grind-and-scratch-and-drop).

Shipman, John. Personal interview by the author. June 24, 2015.

U.S. Glass Online. "Glazier Ranked Nation's 75th-Best Job." July 15, 2013. Retrieved June 23, 2015 (http://www.usglassmag.com/contractglazing/2013/07/15/glazier-ranked-nations-75th-best-job).

U.S. News & World Report. "Glazier." Retrieved June 21, 2015 (http://money.usnews.com/careers/best-jobs/glazier).

index

P

R

S

T

U

W

ABOUT THE AUTHOR

Tamra Orr is a full-time author living in the Pacific Northwest. After receiving her bachelor of science degree in English and education from Ball State University, she began writing full-time for students of all ages. She became interested in glasswork when she and her family moved to a large city and she was surrounded by huge high-rises. As a resident of Portland, Oregon, Orr is surrounded by skyscrapers. When she is not writing, Orr is camping with her husband and children or writing letters to friends around the globe.

PHOTO CREDITS

Cover, p. 1 Ikonoklast Fotografie/Shutterstock.com; pp. 4-5 Ffooter/Shutterstock.com; pp. 8-9 Huntstock/Thinkstock; pp. 10-11 jveal1977/iStock/Thinkstock; p. 13 © iStockphoto.com/igorr1; pp. 14-15 Echo/Cultura/Getty Images; pp. 16-17 Pablo Rogat/Shutterstock.com; pp. 20-21 Jetta Productions/Blend Images/Getty Images; p. 23 unkas_photo/iStock/Thinkstock; p. 25 Laborant/Shutterstock.com; pp. 26-27 Wicki58/E+/Getty Images; p. 28 Eag1eEyes/Shutterstock.com; pp. 30-31 Mikhail Nekrasov/Shutterstock.com; pp. 34-35 Mandel Ngan/AFP/Getty Images; p. 36 Universal History Archive/UIG/Getty Images; p. 40 Knauer/Johnston/Photolibrary/Getty Images; pp. 42-43 Peathegee Inc/Blend Images/Getty Images; pp. 46-47 Hero Images/Getty Images; pp. 48-49 Anadolu Agency/Getty Images; pp. 50-51 TOMO/Shutterstock.com; p. 54 Portland Press Herald/Getty Images; pp. 56-57 Pressmaster/Shutterstock.com; p. 61 Anton Cherstvenkov/iStock/Thinkstock; pp. 62-63 Bloomberg/Getty Images

Designer: Matt Cauli; Editor: Jacob Steinberg; Photo Researcher: Karen Huang